THE LITTLE BOOK OF SELF ESTEEM

Anita Naik

A division of Hachette Children's Books

A Catalogue record for this book is available from
the British Library

ISBN-10: 0 340 93045 4
ISBN-13: 9780340930458

Printed and bound in Great Britain by Bookmarque Ltd, Croydon, Surrey

The paper and board used in this paperback by Hodder Children's Books
are natural recyclable products made from wood grown in
sustainable forests. The manufacturing processes conform to the
environmental regulations of the country of origin.

Hodder Children's Books
a division of Hachette Children's Books
338 Euston Road
London NW1 3BH

For Freya, Nell and Cassie – for
when you're older and maybe
having a bad hair day

You are good enough

Meaning you're good enough just as you are right now. It really doesn't matter what others say about you, or how they feel you should improve yourself. It's only your opinion that counts, so don't let other people put you down or hold you back!

Dare to be different

It's OK to be different from your
friends. Don't be afraid to hold
different opinions, look different
and have different interests. It's
hard to stand out from the
crowd, but if you take a deep
breath, stay true to yourself, and
go for what you want, you'll end
up happy and confident.

Fake it to make it

Even confident people fake
it sometimes. It's only human
to feel anxious, but you don't
have to give in to that wobbly,
shy feeling.

Instead, pretend you can
handle it. Your brain will soon get
the message (the brain believes
what you tell it), and you'll soon
fill up with genuine confidence.

Choose to be happy

You really can decide to be happy. To change your mindset when you're down, think about what makes you laugh and feel warm inside, and remember moments which made you smile. Focus on these feelings and memories, and you'll feel your mood instantly start to lift.

Reinvent yourself

Are you a reflection of what your parents and friends want you to be? If you're feeling desperate to express your true self, change something. It could be your look, what you do after school, or even how you speak up in class. This will boost your confidence and help you emerge from the shadow of other people.

Don't say mean things

If you feel dispirited and low, is it
because you've been saying
mean things? People who say
mean things about others tend to
say even meaner things to
themselves.

Be nicer to yourself
and you'll find you'll instantly
want to be nicer to others.
They'll be nicer back to you,
and the world will be a
brighter place!

Be
your own
cheerleader!

Don't wait for others to tell you that you're great – just decide for yourself. It's not bigheaded to be positive about yourself, and acknowledge your good points. In fact, it's a sign of healthy self-esteem to be able to say, 'I'm great' and mean it.

Like yourself

Stop analysing your flaws and
remind yourself of all the reasons
why you're a good person and a
great friend. You don't have to
be perfect – you just have to be
you. If you're doing that the best
way you can, then you should be
proud of yourself.

Forget about perfection

A tiny bottom, hair that doesn't frizz in the rain, and breasts that are bigger/smaller/more pert? If these are just some of the must-haves on your personal wish list, think again. Body perfection is impossible to achieve, and seeking it just zaps your self-esteem – so let it go!

Implement the anti-moan

You may have good reason to complain, but studies show that constant whining lowers the mood. To break the habit and feel amazing, every time you feel

a moan escaping, follow it up
with an anti-moan: I hate my
legs, but I like my hair; I hate
Mondays, but it's another seven
days until the next one.

Discover your hidden talents

Think you're worthless? Think again. Every single person has talents and strengths. To discover your worth, search for what you're good at, ask friends for their view and look at what you love to do. Value your skills and abilities, because they are more special than you think.

Learn to take compliments

If you can accept the bad things people say, you can accept the positive too. People give compliments because they want you to see the good things about yourself. If you throw them back in their face, all you're doing is teaching them not to say nice things to you in future.

Check who's on your team

We're not talking sports teams, but your personal team. Are your friends, family members and boyfriends for you or against you?

People on your team
should be there because they're
supportive of you. If they're
not on your side, strike them off,
or make sure they shape up.

Use positive body language

Confidence is not just about
what you say, but also about how
you present yourself to the
world. To boost your self-esteem,
make eye contact when people

speak to you, smile when
someone says hello and stand
up straight when speaking. You'll
instantly feel stronger, braver and
more in control.

Perfect your posture

Feeling shy and insecure? Try standing tall – literally. Imagine a string pulling you upwards from the centre of your head, and an opposing one pulling downwards through the centre of your body at the same time.

Now pull your belly button
towards your spine and let your
chest and shoulders relax
and breathe. You should now be
feeling centred and strong.

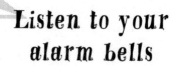

Listen to your alarm bells

Learn to say no to friends with stronger personalities than you, especially if they are encouraging you to do something that feels wrong or strange.

Our internal alarm bells ring
for a reason. Learning to
listen to them will help
you kick back against
peer pressure.

Say things in the positive

Our brain only thinks in positives, so if you say, 'I'm not ugly', the brain will focus on the word 'ugly'. To boost your confidence, use positive language when thinking and talking about yourself.

Think, 'I'm smart' instead of
'I'm not stupid';
'I'm pretty' in place of
'I'm not ugly'
and 'I'm a good person' instead
of 'I'm not that bad'.

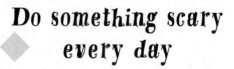

Do something scary every day

Facing one of your fears every day is a guaranteed way to make you feel bold. Start small with fears such as speaking up in class, or saying hello to someone you fancy, and then build on your successes by tackling bigger and bigger fears until you feel you can conquer anything.

Aim high

To have an amazing life, it pays to
aim high. So forget what your
teachers, parents and friends say
about your capabilities. The fact
is, you're capable of anything
you set your mind to, as long as
you're determined to work hard.

Make your weaknesses your strengths

So you're too soft, or too quiet, or too loud? These might feel like weaknesses but they can also be your strengths. 'Too soft' means you're sensitive and intuitive,

'too quiet' means you're a good
listener, and 'too loud' means
you like to stand up for yourself.
Fine-tune your traits by all
means, but don't rubbish them.

Be realistic about love

Love is fantastic, amazing and
the stuff of dreams, but you fall
in love and then . . . life goes on
as normal. Getting a boyfriend
won't suddenly make you feel
happy, confident and attractive if

you don't feel that way already.

So don't expect a boyfriend to

change your self-esteem –

you need to sort that out

for yourself.

Be enthusiastic

So you hate school, loathe boring
nights in with your parents and
can't stand family outings?
Whingeing your way through
them won't make them any

better. So for two weeks,
make yourself be enthusiastic
about everything you do, and
note the difference in how you
feel about your life.

Give yourself a makeover

Dark, baggy clothes don't make anyone feel amazing, so here are three ways to lift your look.

(1) Wear clothes that fit – they will make you look ten times slimmer.
(2) Wear colours that make you feel uplifted – look at a colour spectrum chart to see what appeals to you.
(3) Accentuate your best features so people focus on them when they look at you.

Who dares wins

Dare to take more risks – not
dangerous ones that risk you
being injured or stupid ones that
risk you getting in trouble, but
risks that push you to move out
of your comfort zone. It doesn't

matter if you win or lose –
the more you take a deep breath
and jump in, the stronger and
more confident you will feel
about yourself.

Silence the voice in your head

Do you have a voice in your head that says you can't do things, or you shouldn't try new things? If so, you're not alone. This inner critic is a direct result of the messages we receive from other people, but you can shut it down any time by directly challenging what it says to you. If it says you can't, shout you can. If it says you'll fail, decide to prove that you won't. Fight back each time and slowly but surely the voice will get quieter and quieter.

Move out of 'If only…' land

Many low self esteemers live in 'If only' land. F or example, they think, 'If only I was prettier/ smarter/thinner, I would be happier'. Sadly, this is just a way to avoid dealing with your life face on.

If you hate your body, are you being as healthy as you could be? If you're doing badly at school, who can you ask for help? Focus on the solution, not the problem.

Really Really
look look
at at
yourself yourself

You probably think you look at
yourself every day, but the
chances are you only focus on
the bad points or look at the bits
you like. To improve your body
image, stand in front of the
mirror for two minutes every day.

As you get used to your
reflection you'll find that you'll
stop being so critical and slowly
start to see yourself in a more
positive way.

Make decisions

Believe it or not, you can make
your own decisions about things
like your mood (Am I going to be
happy or miserable today?) or your
personality (Am I going to be an
inspiring person or a
negative one?).

So the next time you
wake up feeling blue, make a
determined decision to be happy
instead of sad, and shake yourself
out of one state and into another.
Try it – it really works!

Ask your friends for help

Feeling blue and down on yourself? Ask your best friends for help. Get them to list your best qualities and remind you of the times you made them laugh or feel better when they were down. Then be sure to do the same for them in return the next time they're feeling depressed.

Do something different today

Read a book you would never
normally pick up, listen to some
music you've always avoided, talk
to someone new, or ask a question
you've never felt able to ask.
Trying something different,
however small, gets you out of your
daily rut and keeps your life
interesting and inspiring.

Stop being a people pleaser

If you find yourself always doing
and saying things to keep your
friends happy, it's time to bring this
to an end. Start being true to
yourself. Real friends will still like
you even if you disagree with them,
say no, or simply stand your ground
over something you believe in.

Beat
shyness

Squash shyness by looking
outwards not inwards. When
you next feel shy, don't agonise
about what people think of you.
Instead, just ask yourself, 'What
do I think of them?'. This will
make you focus on what's
happening and not your
own shyness.

Be grateful

Being grateful doesn't mean
pretending you're happy when
you're not. It means reminding
yourself that, despite the worries,
there are also good things in life.
Every night, before you go to

sleep, write down two things
you were grateful for, such as
having good friends or parents
you get on with, and it will help
you nod off in a more positive
frame of mind.

Identify your influences

There will always be people who make you feel happy in life (the high self-esteemers) and people who make you feel negative (the low self-esteemers). Work out who the negativity vampires are in your life and either challenge what they say to you, or simply stay clear of them.

Stop comparing

Stop comparing yourself to others, especially famous people and supermodels (whose images are retouched by computer) and friends who have different body shapes to you. Make comparisons, and you'll just feel smug or intimidated. Accept that everyone is different, and you are unique!

Be inspiring

It's often tempting to get stuck
into a mutual moaning session
with your friends. Instead, be the
person who encourages and

inspires others to go for what they want. Not only will you be inspired too (it's contagious, you know), but you'll also start to find that you attract similar people who will help lift your life.

Get healthy

If not for the sake of your body
and energy levels, then do it for
your mind.

A healthy diet with lots of fresh
fruit and vegetables alongside
daily exercise not only helps
improve body image
but will also leave you feeling
100% more confident and 100%
more positive.

Make three goals

Having goals to work towards
is essential if you want to feel
confident about your future. So
help yourself by coming up with
three new ones to work towards –

one that will improve how you
feel about yourself;
one to improve how you
feel about your body;
and one to improve how you
feel about your brain power.

Stop feeling guilty

If you regularly feel guilty for not
being a good friend or daughter,
ask yourself this question:

'Should I feel bad, or am I being unreasonable?' Remember, you can only be yourself, not what others expect you to be.

Give in to a laugh

Laughter releases feel-good
hormones known as endorphins
from the brain, so to ensure you
get your fill of these, make sure
you have more fun in your life.

Watch a DVD that makes you roar with laughter, hang out with people who see the funny side of life, and give in to a good giggle whenever you can.

Find a mentor

If you're looking for wise words and
a helping hand, find someone who
has already been there and done
that, as it could be your fast track
to happiness.

A good mentor is
someone older with a broader
vision than you, a person who sees
something special in you, and
above all has the ability to respect
your dreams.

Little things count

If you rarely feel happy, then you need to up your happiness score. Don't wait for large events to transform your life, but learn to recognise the smaller, everyday ones. You might feel better when it's hot and sunny, or when

you're wearing your favourite
shoes, or when a compliment is
thrown your way. Let yourself
really enjoy these little things,
and you'll soon have more to
feel happy about.

Don't choose the dark side

Being cynical and dark

doesn't make you a deeper

or a cleverer person.

What's more, nothing was ever made better by being miserable about it. So make sure your glass is half-full, not half-empty, and start enjoying the upside of life by choosing to see the good in yourself and others.

Stay connected

A sense of belonging brings
happiness and confidence, because
it makes you realise you have a
place in the world. The trick is to
stay connected to your friends and
family during the good times and
the bad, so you get to see they are
with you, no matter what.

Banish your past

The past doesn't have to determine the future unless you let it. Lots of people overcome terrible backgrounds, slurs against their personality and serious mistakes, and you can too. The only thing that matters is what YOU think of you. Step away from the past, live in the present and plan for the future.

Give up toxic worrying

Worrying can be a form of problem solving. It can help you work out where you have gone wrong, or where you might go wrong in a situation. But toxic worrying, where you worry endlessly and go round in circles without sorting

anything out, interferes with your
ability to be happy – so stamp it out
by having a worry diary. Write down
the stuff that keeps bothering
you, look at what you can solve,
then cross out the rest and
forget about it!

Accept that some people are nasty

It's an unspoken truth that some

people are just nasty and rude

and like to take it out on others.

So if someone pushes past you in

a queue, shouts at you for no

reason or gives you a filthy look, don't blame yourself or make yourself feel bad. It's so obviously their problem, not yours.

Shout STOP!

Every time you find yourself falling
back into bad low self-esteem
habits, shout STOP! Take some
deep breaths and immediately
remind yourself of a person who

loves you for yourself, the last
brilliant thing you achieved and the
last fantastic compliment someone
gave you – and revel in feeling
good about yourself.

Learn to forgive

Too often, people won't forgive
someone who has hurt them
because they assume it means
letting them off the hook.

But forgiving someone lets you off
the hook, as it allows you to stop
reliving the event over and over
again. So forgive, and move on.

Question your shyness

Shyness is a learnt behaviour,
which means you can unlearn it
too. As none of us ever does
anything painful unless it gives us
some kind of positive outcome,
you need to work out what being
shy does for you. For instance,

does it make you feel protected
in social situations? If so,
challenge yourself to break out of
your safe little corner – then you
can find out how much better it
feels if you dare to be brave.

Make people feel special

Most people go through life not
feeling very valued, so boost
your friends' self-esteem by
letting them know you hear what
they are saying. Remember
personal facts about them so

they feel that you care enough

to remember, and learn to

listen without interrupting.

You'll be amazed how they

respond to you.

Trust your friends and family

There is a popular idea that your friends and family don't actually tell you the truth and so any nice things they say to make you feel better about yourself don't count. The reality is, if anyone is going to tell you the truth, it's

your family and friends! If in
doubt, think about how you
respond to them when they're
feeling low. Do you lie to them or
tell them something good to
reassure them they are fine?

Have realistic expectations

Having good self-esteem doesn't
mean that you're going to be happy
all the time from now on!

But it does mean that, no matter what bad stuff happens, you'll be able to deal with it, because inside you know you're strong and wise enough to survive anything.